THE GREAT PACIFIC AIR OFFENSIVE OF WORLD WAR II

Volume 3

On Japan's Doorstep 1945

John W. Lambert

Schiffer Military History
Atglen, PA

Dustjacket artwork by Steve Ferguson, Colorado Springs, CO.

THE FLYING CIRCUS OF OKINAWA

In March, 1945, U.S. Navy ace Lt. Eugene Valencia and his "mowing machine" air division of junior grade lieutenants French, Mitchell and Smith, displayed great promise in their first engagements over Tokyo. The following month, Fighting 9 transferred from the USS *Lexington* to the *Yorktown* where the "mowers' tactics would be proved in full. Above the sea off Okinawa, the 'machine' was hailed "Valencia's Flying Circus" as French accumulated eleven victories, Mitchell accounted for ten, and Smith registered six more. "The Circus Boss" more than tripled his own score at twenty-three, concluding their four-month hunting spree, 43.75 victories without loss or injury in their elements, thus to stand down as the premier flight division in the history of American naval aviation. Seen here is the Valencia "mowing machine" division, aka "the Flying Circus", over the west coast of Okinawa as they jettison their drop tanks and wheel about to meet approaching intruders from the north. Their Hellcats display the geometric tactical markings of white triangles previously applied by the crews of the VF-3 who preceded Fighting 9 aboard *Yorktown*. The green prop hubs are a traditional marker as well. Typical of most U.S. Navy carrier based squadrons, Valencia's quartet rarely flew the same Hellcats on successive missions. Likewise, VF-9 crews rarely applied personal markings on their aircraft.

Acknowledgments

We are indebted to the following individuals and organizations for assistance in providing photos and information: Bill Balden, Charles Barr, Dr. John Benbow, Raymond Cole, Jim Crow, John Ebel, John Fitzgerald,Manly Fouts, Hap Halloran, Bill Hess, Jim Hinkle, Bob Ketenheim, Louis Korb, Jim Lansdale, Robert Ley, Bob Louwers, George Lovering, Joe Maita, Ernie McDowell, Robert Moore, Morgan Redwine, Henry Sakaida, Jerry Scutts, Leon Sher, Richard Simms, Don Statsmann, Alec Streete, Lester Twigg, Ernest Thomas, Jim VandeHey, Jim VanNada, Yoji Watanabe, Bill Webster, Hank Weinberger, Jim Weir, Durwood Williams, Dr. Bill Wolf, U.S. National Archives (NARS), Washington, DC; The Museum of Naval Aviation (MNA), Pensacola, FL; U.S. Air Force (USAF), U.S. Navy (USN).

Book design by John W. Lambert.
Cover design by Robert Biondi.

Copyright © 2005 by John W. Lambert.
Library of Congress Catalog Number: 2005924764.

Printed in China.
ISBN: 0-7643-2268-0

We are always looking for people to write books on new and related subjects. If you have an idea for a book, please contact us at the address below.

Published by Schiffer Publishing Ltd.
4880 Lower Valley Road
Atglen, PA 19310
Phone: (610) 593-1777
FAX: (610) 593-2002
E-mail: Info@schifferbooks.com.
Visit our web site at: www.schifferbooks.com
Please write for a free catalog.
This book may be purchased from the publisher.
Please include $3.95 postage.
Try your bookstore first.

In Europe, Schiffer books are distributed by:
Bushwood Books
6 Marksbury Ave.
Kew Gardens
Surrey TW9 4JF
England
Phone: 44 (0)20 8392-8585
FAX: 44 (0)20 8392-9876
E-mail: Bushwd@aol.com.
Free postage in the UK. Europe: air mail at cost.
Try your bookstore first.

FOREWORD

World War II in the Pacific began with an attack by Japanese aircraft carrier units against Oahu on 7 December 1941. From that time until the conclusion of hostilities in August 1945 the conflict was dominated by air power strategy for both the Allies and the Japanese. In the final analysis Allied air power proved decisive in achieving victory

There were no land masses in the broad reaches of the Pacific Ocean where great armies could clash, unlike th
e struggles in North Africa, Eastern Europe or the Western Front. The battles in the adjacent China-Burma-India theater of operations were the sole exception.

By mid 1942 the post Pearl Harbor Japanese juggernaut had reached to Australia and Southeast Asia. The Allies finally held the line, during the aircraft carrier conflicts in the Coral Sea and at Midway and with desperate ground actions in New Guinea and the Solomons Islands, and by 1943 the Japanese were forced on the defensive.

This volume depicts the Allied offensive drive that followed. In this vast region there were no islands where more than a handful of infantry divisions would meet in face-to-face struggles, New Guinea, the Philippines, and Okinawa being the most notable exceptions. In these and other islands ground forces engaged in bitter fighting in appalling terrain under dreadful conditions. But the strategic plan of General Douglas MacArthur and Admiral Chester Nimitz was not to seize territory but airfields or ground that would lend itself to the construction of airfields. They were viewed as the strategic stepping stones to Japan. Aviation engineers often worked under fire to hew new air bases out of jungle, coral, or volcanic rock. With each new airfield complex the range of Allied land-based aircraft was advanced, permitting new areas of Japanese territory to come under air attack.

Even the titanic naval battles of the Pacific were primarily contests between carrier-based forces. Only in a handful of encounters did large fleets of warships engage each other in brief surface gun battles.

In virtually every Pacific campaign, the Allied air forces sought to achieve aerial supremacy, interdict Japanese maritime supply lines, and isolate the battlefield. When this was accomplished enemy ground forces were either destroyed by air power or bypassed. Some Japanese-held islands were never invaded and their garrisons never engaged. They could neither attack nor retreat because of the supremacy of Allied air power Thus they were left to wither in the wake of the advance. With hindsight it became apparent that Allied air power had become so dominant that some islands were invaded needlessly.

The targets of both carrier-based and land-based Allied air forces were largely tactical until the island-hopping strategy allowed B-29 Superforts to begin the final strategic aerial campaign against Japanese home island-industry in late 1944.

Along the path of the Pacific Allied advance air battles never achieved numbers approaching the thousand-plane strategic air raids that were launched from England. Still the air campaigns for domination of the Solomons and New Guinea were fought until the virtual destruction of one air force or the other. Likewise carrier vs. carrier battles generally saw the near annihilation of the losers air groups.

By late 1942 both Japanese and U.S. Navy aircraft carrier units had been dramatically reduced by the early contests: Coral Sea, Midway, Santa Cruz. The Japanese, however, had few carrier replacements while United States shipbuilding capacity began to spawn dozens of new carriers that would scourge the central Pacific with near impunity.

In 1943 the Allies seized the initiative from the Japanese in the Southwest Pacific with victories in New Guinea and the Solomons and began the offensive drive that would breach Japan's Pacific defense ring in the Carolines.

Subsequent carrier battles, such as the First Battle of the Philippine Sea, found hundreds of aircraft engaged on both sides. The Allied approach to the Philippines was a magnet for Japanese reserve squadrons from Formosa, China and the home islands. It was here that the desperate Japanese began to employ Kamikaze tactics.

By the end of 1944 Allied air power had advanced the bomb line to the Japanese homeland, with new c arrier task forces, a continuous string of new island air bases, and new and improved aircraft. Once the air offensive reached Japan hundreds of aircraft clashed in the skies over Kyushu and Honshu.

This is a pictorial history of those intrepid airmen and the aircraft that battled for control of the Pacific Ocean during the great Allied air offensive of World War II..

These photos have been obtained from the private collections of veterans and from various official archives, all noted in "Acknowledgments." Some archival views may have been previously published, since they are in the public domain. Information accompanying official photos was frequently cryptic, incomplete, or incorrect. However, extensive research has provided historically accurate captions unseen in other works.

The reader should keep in mind that these photos, whether taken by professionals with superior cameras or by veterans as amateur snapshots, were all created under less than favorable conditions and have suffered first the ravages of the tropics and then the passage of half a century. Action pictures in particular often have obvious flaws in quality. They can not be staged. Some combat photos were made with hand held cameras, but many were taken by fixed cameras mounted in the tail, wing, or nose of various aircraft. The range of fixed cameras was estimated and set prior to takeoff. Once airborne, the camera was activated by the pilot, but he could not adjust for focus nor worry about positioning the target down sun.

Regardless of any imperfections, these rare photos provide a unique visual record of World War II in the Pacific, a conflict wherein air power proved to be the decisive factor.

CONTENTS

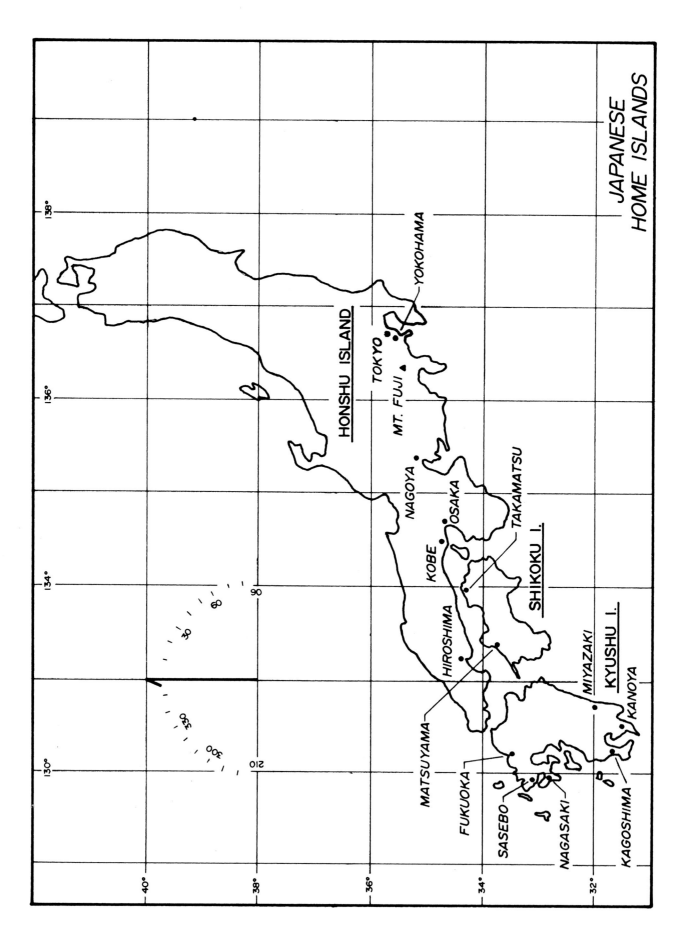

JAPANESE
HOME ISLANDS

HONSHU ISLAND

YOKOHAMA
TOKYO
MT. FUJI
NAGOYA
OSAKA
KOBE
TAKAMATSU
SHIKOKU I.
HIROSHIMA
KYUSHU I.
MIYAZAKI
MATSUYAMA
KANOYA
FUKUOKA
SASEBO
NAGASAKI
KAGOSHIMA

138°
136°
134°
130°

40°
38°
36°
34°
32°

1

OKINAWA AND IE SHIMA:
THE UNSINKABLE AIRCRAFT CARRIERS

Okinawa and its tiny neighbor, Ie Shima, turned out to be the last "island hopping" operation of the Pacific war. The bitter struggle for these two locations was consistent with the MacArthur-Nimitz strategy of seizing ground to advance land-based aircraft ever closer to the enemy center. Formosa, the coast of China, and the Dutch East Indies were all bypassed in favor of the Ryukyu Islands. Air bases in this chain put even fighter aircraft within 300 miles of Japan's southernmost island, Kyushu

Marine Air Groups 31 and 32 arrived on Okinawa between the 7th and 9th of April 1945 as the ground battle still raged. These Corsair equipped squadrons were immediately pressed into the action against Japanese air units, intent on sinking ships of the invasion fleet. They were followed by MAGs 22 and 14 and by AAF units that formed the Tactical Air Force under Marine direction. This command was assigned the primary mission of neutralizing the Ryukyu chain and extending the war to Kyushu

The first AAF squadrons, from the 318th Fighter Group, arrived on 13 May 1945, equipped with the new Republic P-47N, the ultimate version of the Thunderbolt line. It was an aircraft with enormous range capability. The 318th had their share of fighting Japanese raiders but were soon sending sorties against

the home island of Kyushu on both night interdiction and daylight strikes.

Two more P-47N units, the 413th and 507th Fighter Groups, arrived by late June to join the Tactical Air Force. The Seventh Air Force would add its 41st, 319th, 494th and 11th Bomb Groups to the mix. The Fiifth Air Force, coming from the Philippines, joined the fight in July and August with four veteran fighter units and five bomb groups. This concentration of air power created traffic jams on the airfields and in the skies around Okinawa. None-the-less, the joint force heaped misery on Kyushu which was being overwhelmed with day and night sweeps and bombing missions by the AAF legions.

There were sporadic night raids against the Allied air bases on Okinawa and Ie Shima, but the Japanese lacked the strategic bomber forces to alter the course of events. They could not sink the land-based airfields, and thus focused on destroying ships that would be employed in the coming invasion of Japan.

While Marianas-based B-29s concentrated their effort against the industrial cities of Honshu, the Tactical Air Force attempted to destroy Japanese air strength and received many target assignments that would facilitate OPERATION OLYMPIC, the pending invasion of Kyushu.

Above: Ie Shima, the last beachhead of World War II, is a tiny island just two miles west of Okinawa. Only five miles long and relatively flat, it was invaded on 1 April 1945 primarily for of its airfield potential. The Japanese already had a 3,700 foot coral runway there, and aviation engineers set about improving it and building three more runways along with taxiways and hardstands. The finished product is seen here. (Author's Collection)

AT THIS SPOT
THE 77ª INFANTRY DIVISION
LOST A BUDDY
ERNIE PYLE
18 APRIL 1945

Left: Termed "the last damned island," by ground troops, Ie Shima was where war correspondent Ernie Pyle met his death. (Author's Collection)

Above: The night skies over Okinawa were periodically illuminated by the arcs of tracers fired from the AA batteries of ships and shore based artillery. This frequently published scene, taken from Yontan A/D, illustrates one such event. When the AA came back to earth, it killed and injured many Allied personnel. They huddled in slit trenches more for protection from their own defensive fire than from Japanese raiders. (USMC)

Below: An air raid on offshore shipping seen from the 318th Fighter Group tent camp on Ie Shima. A Kamikaze has just plunged into a ship (center) after avoiding the flak of many AA guns. (Jim Weir)

Okinawa's early night air defense was provided by several Marine squadrons flying the radar-equipped Grumman F6F-5N Hellcat.

Above: A Hellcat of VMF(N)-533. This squadron scored 35 night kills, leading all Marine night units. (NARS)

Below: The top scoring ace of VMF(N)-533, Captain Robert Baird (right), who downed six night raiders, is congratulated by Marine Major General Louis Woods. (NARS)

The 303rd Hikotai, of the 203rd Naval Air Group, was equipped with the Zero (Zeke) Model 52 as pilots pose here in the Spring of 1945. They participated in Okinawa operations and then the defense of Kyushu against the U.S. Navy, Marines and AAF. (Henry Sakaida)

Among aces serving with the 203rd Naval Air Group were: (l. to r.) WO Takeo Tanamizu and Lt. (jg) Tetsuzo Iwamoto. Tanamizu was a veteran of Rabaul and Taiwan before his final combat over the Homeland. He claimed eighteen kills. Iwamoto, who first flew in combat over China in 1938, and subsequently fought in carrier battles and at island bases throughout the Pacific, may have been Japan's leading ace. He claimed 202 aerial victories. Both survived the war. (Henry Sakaida)

The 318th Fighter Group was equipped with the new Republic P-47N and was the first AAF unit to operate from Ie Shima, arriving on 13 May 1945. The operating range of the dash N over the original model increased from 400 to near 1,000 miles as internal fuel capacity increased from 305 to 556 gallons. It had more power and more speed than the P-47D along with a new gunsight and automatic pilot, and many other improved features. It was theorized that the P-47N could operate deep into Japan from Ie Shima. Colonel Lew Sanders, CO of the 318th and a Pearl Harbor vet, is seen here with a new N. (Author's Collection)

The ability of the Thunderbolt to carry enormous payloads is demonstrated in this view of GLORY GAL, a P-47N-1-RE of the 73rd Squadron, 318th Fighter Group. She is loaded with three 500-pounders and 10 rockets. The 318th also tried 300 gallon auxiliary wing tanks. (Author's Collection)

Before runways could be lengthened and the surfaces improved, the short dusty coral strip on Ie Shima cost the loss of several aircraft and some pilots. The range potential of the P-47N caused Tactical Air Force commanders to test its limits. This 318th P-47N burns after a takeoff crash that killed the pilot. (Author's Collection)

The name on this P-47N of the 333rd Squadron, 318th Fighter Group was TOO BIG TOO HEAVY, reflecting the pilot's view of takeoff perils in the fully loaded Thunderbolt from Ie Shima's relatively short runways. The 318th tried auxiliary wing tanks of up to 300-gallon capacity. Artist and pilot was Lieutenant John Brunner. (Author's Collection)

The flight line of the 333rd Fighter Squadron. The P-47N LANDLUBBER IV has been opened for maintenance. (Joe Maita)

Left: On 25 May 1945, returning from a Kyushu mission aborted because of weather, the 318th Fighter Group ran into a formation of Japanese raiders bound for Okinawa. The Thunderbolt pilots engaged and destroyed over 30 Japanese aircraft. 1st Lieutenant Richard H. Anderson (left), 19th Squadron, downed five Zekes, in his one and only aerial engagement. Center is flight surgeon, Captain A.D. McKinley and Captain Bill Loflin is at the right. Loflin, who had a kill flying a P-38 near Iwo Jima, downed a pair of Japanese fighters over Kanoya A/D, Kyushu on 10 June 1945. (Author's Collection)

Captain John Vogt, 19th Squadron, 318th Fighter Group, downed five Japanese fighters over Kyushu on 28 May 1945. (Jim Weir)

The P-47N of Captain Judge Wolfe, 333rd Squadron. After downing two Bettys over Iwo Jima in a P-38, Wolfe got one Kamikaze over the Ryukyu chain and six Japanese fighters over Kyushu. Leading ace of the 318th Fighter Group, he was killed in a flying accident three years after the war. (Joe Maita)

Flying escort to a Navy photo recon aircraft off Kyushu on 10 June 1945, the 318th Fighter Group attracted many Japanese fighters.

Above: Lieutenant Durwood B. Williams, firing from short range, downed a Zeke (as seen in the gun camera clip at the right), then a Jack, which exploded, resulting in damage to the leading edge of Williams' right wing. (D.B. Williams)

Below: Durwood Williams is seen in his 333rd Squadron P-47N with unit insignia and victory flags. (D.B. Williams)

Right: A 318th Fighter Group mission over Southern Kyushu was jumped by Japanese fighters On 7 June 1945. 2nd Lieutenant Ellis Wallenberg's P-47 was hit, his canopy blown off, his engine damaged and a cannon round passed through one propeller blade. Despite a gash on his forehead and a rough engine, Wallenberg nursed his P-47 back toward Ie Shima. With oil finally gone and engine dying, the 73rd Squadron pilot stretched his glide and landed on Ie Shima. Here he examines the hole in his prop. Young Lieutenant Wallenberg expended all of his luck on this mission. On 10 July, after strafing Amami Oshima to protect a rescue PBM, Wallenberg developed engine trouble. He was seen to parachute but fell to his death. (NARS)

Left: 1st Lieutenant John Dooling of the 333rd Squadron, 318th Fighter Group, marvels at the strength of his damaged Republic Thunderbolt that brought him back to base. Japanese flak tore away this huge section of right wing while he was strafing in the Ryukyu chain in July 1945. (NARS)

THE WITTLE WAMPIRE, P-47N, 333rd Squadron, 318th Fighter Group. (Joe Maita)

P-47N KILLER'S DILLER II and pilot Lieutenant Don Kane, 73rd Squadron, 318th Fighter Group. (Author's Collection)

The 507th Fighter Group, last of the new AAF fighter units to reach Ie Shima, began operations on 30 June 1945. SHELL PUSHER was from the 463rd Squadron, denoted by the triangle on the tail. (Bill Hess)

Japanese attacks on Okinawa and the adjacent fleet tapered off but never ended. Night raiders caused minimal damage but kept the forces ashore and afloat awake. The 548th Night Fighter Squadron was shifted from Iwo Jima to Ie Shima in May 1945 to assist in the air defense.

Above: This is a P-61 of the 548th with drop tanks which allowed additional "hover" time. The 548th bagged five Japanese night attackers between June and August. (Author's Collection)

Below: BAT OUT'A HELL scored a night victory over a Rufe on 22 June 1945. The pilot was Captain Bill Dames; radar operator, 2nd Lieutenant Gene Dandrea; and observer, Sergeant Ray Ryder. (Author's Collection)

The Martin PBM Mariner was the ultimate in World War II flying boat development and slowly replaced the venerable Catalina. It attained barely 200 mph maximum speed, but was blessed with an operating range of 1400 miles.

Above: A PBM-5 of VP-21 has had its tail damaged by flak near the China Coast. (NARS)

Below: SEXY ANNA, another Mariner of VPB-21, took some hits off the coast of Korea. Returning to Kerama Retto, it is about to be lifted aboard the seaplane tender, *Chandeleur*. The bubble above the cockpit houses the search radar. (Richard Simms)

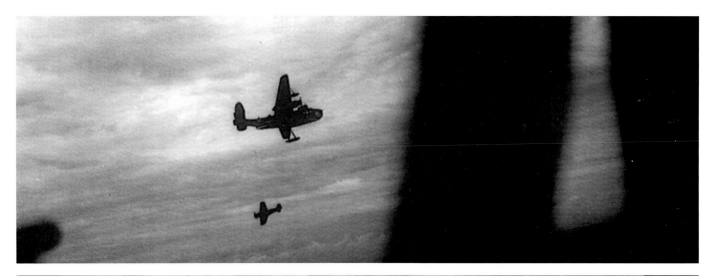

Top: On 14 May 1945, off the west coast of Japan, seven Oscars attacked a pair of VPB-21 Mariners. A close pass by one of the Japanese fighters as seen from another PBM. (Richard Simms)

Center: One of the Japanese fighters dropped a phosphorous bomb which did no harm. However, the PBM of Richard Simms was damaged by machine gun rounds and obliged to ditch. (Richard Simms)

Lower: Spotted by Marine Corsairs the following day, Simms and crew were recovered by a Mariner of rescue squadron VH-1 that made a water landing. (Richard Simms)

Above: A Consolidated PB4Y-2 Privateer of VPB-123 on Okinawa. By early 1945, the Dash 2 Privateers had replaced Dash 1 Liberators among USN squadrons. (Author's Collection)

Below: On 29 July 1945 this 1,300-ton freighter was attacked and sunk by Okinawa-based Privateers of Fleet Air Wing One. The action took place southeast of Pusan, Korea. Note that AA guns above the bridge have been abandoned. (MNA)

After pre-invasion mapping of Iwo Jima, 28th Photo Recon Squadron, Lockheed F-5Bs added many missions mapping Kyushu and Honshu for the invasion that was never launched.

Above: MISSOURI OUTLAW shows 71 mission symbols. (Jim Crow)

Below: A 28th Photo Recon F-5B Lightning and a Curtiss Commando C-46 transport had a disastrous but not fatal ground collision. The name on the C-46 is REARIN' TO GO. (Jim Crow)

Japanese raiders continued to attack Okinawa, Ie Shima and the fleet in surrounding waters until the final day of the war, although in ever diminishing numbers. 2nd Lieutenant Stuart Alley, Jr. of VMF-323 downed five enemy aircraft, including three Vals on 3 June 1945. (NARS)

The 348th Fighter Group, Fifth Air Force, converted from their P-47 Thunderbolts to North American Mustangs after arriving in the Philippines. They advanced to Okinawa on 14 July 1945 when airfield space finally became available but saw only modest aerial combat. JOSIE is the P-51K-10 of ace, Captain Mike Dikovitsky. (Bill Hess)

Mitchells of the 41st Bomb Group tested the use of glide torpedoes. Here a pair of dash Js depart from Okinawa for Sasebo, Kyushu on 28 July 1945. (NARS)

Fifth Air Force Liberators began to arrive on Okinawa 30 July 1945. They flew only a few missions before the war ended. Airfield congestion required these 380th Bomb Group B-24s to line up nose to tail. After VJ-Day they flew supply missions to POW camps in Japan. (Author's Collection)

The 345th Bomb Group arrived on Ie Shima on 30 July 1945 in time for a few shipping strikes in the Straits of Tsushima, between Japan and Korea, and raids on Kyushu.

Above: TIM N' TAM (named for Lieutenant Tom Fitzpatrick's twins) was a 499th Squadron dash J, SN 44-30350. (Joe Maita)

Below: A B-25J of the 498th Squadron. (Author's Collection)

Above: The Douglas A-26 Invader, a new light bomber of A-20 Havoc lineage, had just arrived in the Pacific on Okinawa on 8 July 1945. The 41st Bomb Group began to convert from their B-25 Mitchells. (NARS)

Below: The veteran 3rd Bomb Group arrived on Okinawa on 29 July 1945 and had begun to convert from the A-20 to the new A-26. This war weary A-20 of the 89th Squadron bellied in after a mission to Kyushu. (NARS)

Above: By July engineers had extended le Shima's runways to 5,600 feet. Still it took a lot to get the heavily loaded P-47N into the humid, air as noted by Captain Alec Streete: "Eight tons of nuts and bolts, 80 inches of manifold pressure, and full throttle." Streete is seen here in his 463rd Squadron, 507th Fighter Group aircraft being guided to takeoff by a member of his ground crew. (Alec Streete)

Left: CHAUTAUQUA PRINCESS was a P-47N2-RE of the 463rd Squadron, 507th Fighter Group, shown here on le Shima in August 1945. (Author's Collection)

Above: 1st Lieutenant Oscar Perdamo (left), 464th Squadron, 507th Fighter Group bagged five Japanese aircraft on 13 August 1945 when the 507th flew a 1,580 mile round-trip sweep from Ie Shima to Korea. Intercepted by some 50 Japanese aircraft, the group claimed 20 victories and lost one, its pilot later rescued. Perdamo became the last AAF ace of World War II. (Ernie McDowell)

Right: The veteran 8th Fighter Group, Fifth Air Force, did not arrive on Ie Shima with its P-38Ls until 8 August 1945. It had just one encounter in the closing hours of the war on 14 August 1945. While escorting rescue aircraft over the Inland Sea of Japan, 35th Squadron Lightnings were jumped by Japanese fighters. They downed five Nakajima Ki-84 Franks but lost one of their own, Lieutenant Duane L. Keiffer. He was one of the last AAF casualties of World War II. (Jim Crow)

VMF-323, nicknamed "Death Rattlers," flew Corsairs in the defense of Okinawa and on offensive missions as far north as Kyushu. In two months of operations they tallied 124.5 aerial victories. Here is a group picture of its aces and their individual scores: (l. to r.) Major Jeff Dorroh (6); 2nd Lieutenant Stuart Alley (5); 1st Lieutenant Albert Wells (5); 1st Lieutenant Francis Terrill (6.5); 2nd Lieutenant Bill Drake (5); 1st Lieutenant Joe Dillard (6.33); 1st Lieutenant Jerry O'Keefe (7); 2nd Lieutenant Dewey Durnford (6.33); 1st Lieutenant Bill Hood (5.5). Not present at the time of the photo are aces, John Ruhsam (7); and Robert Wade (7). (Bill Wolf)

A far-ranging Mariner of VPB-27 from Okinawa searches the coast of China in the closing days of the war. (USN)

2

THE STRATEGIC AIR OFFENSIVE AGAINST JAPAN

In 1943 Allied planners projected an aerial assault against the Japanese home islands, in the same manner that the U.S. Eighth Air Force and the RAF were then bombing Germany and occupied Europe. At that point in the war they were thousands of miles from the enemy heartland without an aircraft capable of fulfilling the scheme. Visionary AAF leaders had anticipated the need of a very long range heavy bomber and commenced design and development of such an aircraft in 1939. The end product was the Boeing B-29 Superfortress, an aircraft that dwarfed the four-engined Boeing B-17 and Consolidated B-24. Apart from its sheer size, the Superfortress could carry a credible bomb load and return over a 3,000 mile route. It was first flown in September 1942 and by mid 1944 an armada of B-29s was being marshaled for what would become the Twentieth Air Force. Allied advances in the Pacific provided the bases.

Initial raids were mounted from China by 58th Bomb Wing B-29s in June 1944. The balance of the Twentieth began arriving in the Marianas Islands in October 1944, and were joined there by the 58th Bomb Wing in April 1945. The force eventually grew to twenty-five groups, nearly 1,000 B-29s. Bases for the Superfort units, with 8,500 foot runways, were constructed on Saipan, Tinian and Guam.

After some practice missions against Truk and Iwo Jima, first strikes against Honshu from the Marianas were flown in late November 1944, target: Tokyo. The 2,600 mile round trips provided unexpected problems. Takeoffs of fully loaded B-29s were harrowing even on the long runways. However, formations flying at 25,000 to 35,000 feet, experienced a phenomenon that had never been anticipated. The jet stream, which scientists identified in postwar years, was an area of intense winds between polar and mid latitude ranges. It fostered winds of 100 to near 300 knots from

various directions making bombing approaches mere guess work for aircraft with a cruising speed of 230 mph. On more than one occasion, the Superfort crews were astounded to find that ground speed fell away dramatically nearing Honshu. They were hovering, like albatross, in the head winds. Mission logs showed twelve and fifteen hours of air time. Some bomber crews, their fuel spent fighting the hurricane force winds, ditched short of the Marianas. A few missions were aborted because of weather conditions.

Initial planning had sought to target heavy industry: steel mills, aircraft and engine factories, port facilities. But the lack of precision from high altitude contributed to what was generally considered poor results. Enemy flak and fighters were not a major factor for the high altitude formations. Japanese fighters staggered about in the thin air, at the limits of performance, and because of shabby radio equipment and a lack of coordination between their air force and navy, the attacks lacked impact.

The combination of weather problems and poor bombing results compelled a change in tactics in March 1945. By this time weather hunters were being sent ahead of the bombing missions. And by attacking from lower altitude, the fiercest of the head winds were avoided and bombing efficiency soared. The Twentieth Air Force also began using incendiary bombs on urban targets and found that the lightly constructed Japanese cities burned also destroying adjacent industrial targets.

On the night of 9-10 March 1945 a force of 279 B-29s bombed Tokyo from between 5,000 and 9,000 feet. Fourteen were lost, including five that ditched en route home, but the raid caused a fire storm that burned 15.8 square miles of the Imperial Capitol and killed over 83,000 people. Similar devastation was in turn visited on the major cities of Nagoya, Osaka and Kobe.

Attacks on Japanese industrial targets continued along with raids on Kyushu and Shikoku Island airfields that fed Japanese air units into the Okinawa campaign. In addition B-29s began mining the Inland Sea, the Straits of Shimonoseki (between Honshu and Kyushu), and various coastal harbors.

Battling against the B-29 onslaught, Japanese fighter forces from both navy and air force units began to achieve greater success in February 1945. In addition to mass fighter attacks, the Japanese began to employ twin-engined Ki-45, cannon-equipped aircraft against the giant Superforts. Taking a page from the Special Attack Units, some pilots even resorted to ramming tactics.

The B-29 crews ultimately paid a heavy price, but the destruction they wrought on the Japanese war-making potential was awesome by comparison. The delivery of a pair of atomic bombs on Hiroshima and Nagasaki on 6 and 9 August 1945, effectively crushing Japan's will to continue the war, was anti-climactic. Japan's industry had been devastated before these historic events.

The flight deck of a giant Boeing B-29 shows the dual controls and the view (upper center) toward the bombardier's nose station. (Bill Webster)

B-29 Superfortresses had four Wright R-3350-23 engines, each developing 2200 hp, and cruised toward their Japanese targets at 230 mph. Each group had distinctive tail markings. This B-29 is from the 6th Bomb Group. (Bill Webster)

Mount Fujiyama, a striking landmark just southwest of Tokyo, is seen through the nose of a 499th Bomb Group B-29. (Hap Halloran)

The Marianas Islands reverberated to the thunder of an assembling mission.

Above: OILY BOID, and other 29th Bomb Group B-29s, taxi for takeoff on Guam. (Author's Collection)

Below: B-29s took off for missions one after the other, on a closely timed basis. Here TIMMID VIRGIN, with its 8,800 horsepower revved to maximum, awaits the signal of a 29th Bomb Group officer. (Author's Collection)

It was a major physical effort for pilot and co-pilot to lift a fully loaded B-29 off the runway. Here goes a 29th Bomb Group Superfort, 70 tons of aircraft, gasoline, and bombs. (Author's Collection)

A formation of 19th Bomb Group B-29s drop their high explosive bombs in unison over Honshu in mid-1945. (Jim Crow)

Army engineers and Navy construction battalions built vast airfield complexes along with housing and maintenance facilities in the Marianas for the Twentieth Air Force's Bomber Command.

Above: This is a B-29's view of the four parallel 8,500-foot runways on Tinian constructed for the 313th Bomb Wing. (Bill Webster)

Below: The extra long runways were not always adequate for the takeoff of heavily laden B-29s, nor were they always sufficient for landings of battle damaged aircraft or those with mechanical problems. This 501st Bomb Group B-29 crashed on landing at Tinian. (Bill Webster)

The 19th Bomb Group B-29, CITY OF FLATBUSH, like most B-29s, was crewed by a cross section of young Americans: (standing, l. to r.) Jack Tyrell, tail gunner, New York City; Eugene Vick, radio operator, Ellijay, GA; Don Comer, gunner, Birmingham, AL; Don Leeper, engineer, CA; Jack Matthews, radar operator, Milwaukee, WI; Gerson Lacoff, bombardier, Detroit, MI; Gene Victor, navigator, New York City; Jim Hall, aircraft commander, Dallas, TX; Francis Thompson, copilot, Sioux Falls, SD; (kneeling, l. to r.) Leonard Naymark, gunner, Duluth, MN; Marvin Beattie, gunner, Rochester, NY. (Robert Ley)

Bombs for MAXIMUM EFFORT, 19th Bomb Group, await loading on Guam. (Robert Ley)

In January 1945 a Japanese fighter shot out the left waist blister on AMERICAN MAID, a B-29 of the 497th Bomb Group. Sergeant James Krantz, the gunner, was sucked through the opening and dangled from a safety strap for several minutes before crew members could recover him. Krantz survived the experience but had to be treated for severe frost bite. Most B-29s were armed with twelve .50 caliber machine guns in turrets sighted from blisters. This version also mounted a 20 mm cannon in the tail. (NARS)

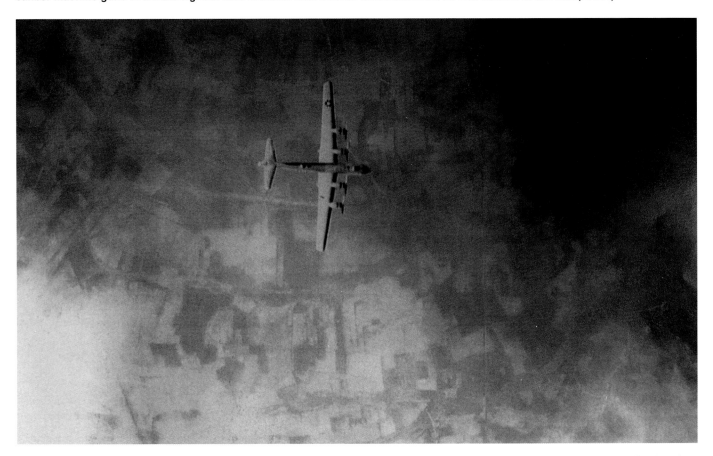

A 499th Bomb Group B-29, ROVER BOYS EXPRESS, falls from formation over Honshu on 27 January 1945, its No. 4 engine burning. The plane had been attacked by Captain Isamu Kashiide's Ki-45 Nick and taken fatal cannon hits. Some crewmen of the Superfort were killed, others parachuted from 27,000 feet into minus 58 degree air. Only five survived brutal captivity. (Hap Halloran)

Above: The twin-engined Kawasaki Ki-45C Toryu (Nick) was no match against Allied single-seat fighters, but its specialized heavy armament proved deadly against B-29s which could otherwise take considerable punishment. This one, captured in the Philippines, is believed to have served with the 5th Hiko Sentai. The Dash C model was a night fighter with a pair of 20mm guns mounted between the front and rear compartments at a 30 degree angle. The muzzles can be seen protruding just aft of the forward canopy (NARS)

Below: This view, with the nose cone removed, shows the Nick's forward firing cannon. A 37mm weapon, it held just twenty rounds, but one well placed shot could down a B-29. (NARS)

A twin-engined Japanese fighter, narrowly missing a collision, dives through a formation of the 29th Bomb Group over Japan. Note the smoke created by the guns of the tail turrets, firing at other Japanese interceptors. (NARS)

Captain Isamu Kashide first saw aerial combat against the Russians in the 1938 Nomonhon border clash where he claimed several kills. In defense of Honshu he flew the Ki-45 Nick with the 4th Sentai and is acknowledged as the premier killer of B-29s with at least seven victories. (Henry Sakaida)

Serving with the 51st Sentai, WO Tadeo Sumi flew the Ki-61 Tony on many missions against B-29 raiders. He is believed to have downed five, including four during a night action over Osaka on 13 March 1945. His final claims were five B-29s, one P-51 destroyed and four B-29s damaged. (Henry Sakaida)

This battle-damaged 500th Bomb Group B-29 was attempting to land on Saipan with two sputtering engines. At the last minute the pilot tried to set her down on the beach. The aircraft nosed over just offshore, and rescuers flocked to the wreck. They assisted most of the injured crew members, but three men trapped in the nose died. (NARS)

Incendiary bombs cascade from the belly of a 39th Bomb Group B-29. Japanese urban areas were highly flammable due to the use of wood and paper in construction. (Bill Webster)

Even before the battle for the island had ended, Iwo Jima became a haven for B-29s returning from missions over Honshu. Ultimately, over 2,000 B-29s sought refuge on Iwo. The runways were shorter than those in the Marianas and crash landings were not infrequent.

Above: A B-29 of the 504th Bomb Group crash-landed on Iwo Jima in April 1945, careening into an embankment. (Author's Collection)

Below: A 500th Bomb Group B-29 just missed a line of 21st Fighter Group Mustangs as it crash-landed on Iwo Jima in May 1945. (Author's Collection)

Above: AMERICAN BEAUTY, a China veteran of the 468th Bomb Group, made it back to Iwo Jima for a crash landing but was too badly damaged to be repaired. (Author's Collection)

Below: This B-29 reached Iwo, but with a damaged landing gear, the pilot elected to ditch just off shore. (Author's Collection)

On 14 May 1945 the Twentieth Air Force delivered one of the largest air raids of the Pacific war with 472 Superfortresses. The target was Nagoya and surprisingly strong Japanese resistence caused the loss of eleven B-29s.

This battle-damaged 19th Bomb Group B-29 (shown in two views) delivered its crew to Iwo Jima but broke in half as a result of the crash landing. (Jim Crow)

BC·5M·187·132V·11·1·JUNE·1050·6"·18,500 ... 4°N·136·45E·OSAKA·5949·12¼°F

In June 1945 this disabled B-29 veered out of formation perilously close to another of the 6th Bomb Group. Note the shadow of the photo plane. Smoke rises from Osaka. 18,000 feet below. (Bill Webster)

REAMATROID, a B-29 of the 6th Bomb Group, is the backdrop for this display of aerial reconnaissance cameras. The aircraft sports 37 mission symbols and one kill flag. (Bill Webster)

A Japanese naval base is photographed by a high flying F-13 (B-29 recon version) prior to a strike. (Bill Webster)

Above: The entire crew walked away from this devastating crash landing. Captain James Pearson flew a round trip of 17 hours, nursing his damaged 500th Bomb Group B-29 back to Saipan with two engines gone on the left side. (NARS)

Below: Flak damage to B-29 SN 42-93846 over Honshu on 16 July 1945 nearly took off the tail of this 504th Bomb Group aircraft. Despite the lack of a rudder, the pilot returned her to Tinian. (Jim Crow)

WHITE MISTRESS, SN 42-24776, 6th Bomb Group, was wrecked when it went off the runway on Tinian. (Jim Crow)

GRAVEL GERTIE, a 500th Bomb Group veteran of 49 missions, crashed on takeoff 6 August 1945, but the crew survived. (NARS)

On 6 August 1945 a single atomic bomb was dropped over Hiroshima in southern Honshu. The 509th Composite Group, led by Colonel Paul W. Tibbetts, Jr., had trained solely for atomic bomb missions.

Above: ENOLA GAY, Tibbetts' B-29, SN 44-86292. This aircraft has been preserved and is on display at the National Air & Space Museum, Dulles Airport. (Author's Collection)

Below: THE GREAT ARTISTE, SN 44-27353, was one of two observer aircraft on the Hiroshima mission. It carried scientific instruments to record the bomb blast. (Bill Webster)

The Boeing B-29 was the last in the World War II line of four-engined bombers with sufficient fuselage for major art. The nose art ran the gamut from mundane to exotic. In the final days of the war some unit commanders banned the nudes as inappropriate. Some art efforts are shown here and on the succeeding pages of this chapter.

MAXIMUM LOAD, SN 42-63563, 9th Bomb Group, is prepped for a mission. The four-gun top turret cover has been removed for servicing, and the barrels are swabbed. (Author's Collection)

SPEAGLE EAGLE of the 6th Bomb Group and a rare female visitor, likely a nurse or USO performer. (Bill Webster)

DAUNTLESS DOTTY, SN 42-24592, 497th Bomb Group, led the first tokyo raid from the Marianas. She completed her tour of duty but crashed on Kwajalein while returning to the U.S. (Author's Collection)

THUNDERBIRD, 29th Bomb Group, was one of the last B-29s lost when the crew bailed out on 8 August 1945. (Author's Collection)

LUCKY LADY, SN 42-24863, 462nd Bomb Group, on Tinian. (Jim Crow)

FAST COMPANY, 468th Bomb Group, on Tinian. (Jim Crow)

T.N. TEENY, SN 44-69920, 9th Bomb Group, on Iwo Jima. (Author's Collection)

SLICK'S CHICKS (shown above and below) was lost with its entire 505th Bomb Group crew in a mid-air collision on 10 February 1945. The emblem honors a Navy construction battalion. (Jim Crow)

SKY SCRAPPER, 497th Bomb Group, was destroyed on Saipan by a Japanese air raid. (Jim Crow)

MILLION DOLLAR BABY, 500th Bomb Group. (Author's Collection)

OUR BABY, 497th Bomb Group, on Saipan. (Author's Collection)

This 502nd Bomb Group B-29 ran off the end of a runway on Iwo Jima. The emblem reads, "Hellbirds: With Malice Toward Some." (Author's Collection)

JOLTIN' JOSIE, SN 42-24614, 498th Bomb Group, crashed on takeoff from Saipan, 1 April 1945, killing the entire crew. (Author's Collection)

JOKERS WILD and crew, 497th Bomb Group, were lost over Nagoya on 3 January 1945. (Author's Collection)

The Coffman crew and DEVIL'S DELIGHT, 500th Bomb Group. (Jim Crow)

DRAGGIN' LADY, SN 42-24694, 500th Bomb Group, ditched on 23 February 1945. (Jim Crow)

MYAS' DRAGON, a B-29 of the 6th Bomb Group (Bill Webster)

PEACE ON EARTH, SN 442-63412, 497th Bomb Group, was ditched on 4 March 1945 returning from Tokyo. Two crewmen were lost. (Jim Crow)

JACKPOT, SN 42-24797, 505th Bomb Group, ditched on 19 March 1945 after a night mission to Nagoya, and her crew was rescued after three days at sea. (Jim Crow)

This 40th Bomb Group B-29 was named for a hospital ship hit by a Kamikaze off Okinawa on 28 April 1945. (Jim Crow)

CHICAGO QUEEN, like all of the B-29s in the 16th Bomb Group, had a black belly. (Jim Crow)

Led by a B-29 Superfortress, the 15th Fighter Group wings north toward Honshu. The presence of the bomber relieved the Mustang pilots of navigation chores. But on the return flight, P-51 pilots who became separated had to find a B-29 to lead the way or navigate by their wits. (USAF)

3

MUSTANGS OVER HONSHU

From its inception, the plan to seize Iwo Jima had two goals: providing a haven for damaged B-29s and establishing a base for AAF fighters that could escort the bombers. The Marianas gave the Superforts a home 1300 miles from Tokyo. But no fighter of that day could make such a round trip. It was, however, theoretically possible for the North American P-51D to fly from Iwo Jima to Tokyo and other southern cities in Honshu, but it was by no means a routine flight.

The Mustang had proved itself over Europe on five and six hour missions that covered 1200 to 1300 miles. However, the Empire run was entirely over-water. After navigating nearly 650 miles to the coast of Japan on rigid cruise control, these pilots would be expected to drop their auxiliary tanks, engage an enemy, and return over the same empty ocean to find Iwo Jima. A mistake of a degree in navigation spelled disaster. Engine trouble, fuel starvation or battle damage requiring a parachute jump would, likewise, force a pilot into the vast Pacific.

The veteran Seventh Fighter Command had trained for this very long range (VLR) role, and its 15th and 21st Fighter Groups had been equipped with the P-51D in Hawaii. Ground echelons landed on Iwo Jima as the battle raged. The first Mustangs (15th Fighter Group) arrived from Saipan at Airfield No. 1, below Mt. Suribachi, on 6-7 March 1945 and immediately began close support for the Marines plus interdiction missions to surrounding islands of the Bonin Group. Airfield No. 2, was cleared and the 21st Fighter Group advanced to Iwo Jima on 25 March.

The island had been declared "secure," and the Marines were withdrawing. But Japanese soldiers still lurked in the labyrinth of underground structures, and in the pre-dawn of 26 March 1945 some 300 of them struck the camp of the 21st Fighter Group and the nearby 549th Night Fighter Squadron. Pilots and ground crews fought with pistols and Carbines until a contingent of troops arrived to help annihilate the enemy force. Even before flying a combat mission, the aviation units had lost 16 killed and 50 wounded.

The first VLR mission to Tokyo was conducted on 7 April 1945 by 96 P-51s which escorted 103 Superforts of the 73rd Bomb Wing. As Japanese fighters engaged the raiders, over 300 aircraft converged in the sky above Honshu. Flak claimed two bombers and fighters downed another, but the Mustangs scored heavily claiming 21 victories, six probables and six damaged for the loss of one of their own. Returning P-51 pilots logged seven and one-quarter hours and were so cramped from confinement that they had to be assisted from their cockpits The arduous effort had been a historic operation, but one that had to be duplicated again and again until 14 August 1945, the last VLR mission.

In May 1945 the Mustang-equipped 506th Fighter Group arrived from the States where they had trained for VLR operations. By this time Japanese defenders rarely attacked the B-29s in daylight and almost never engaged the Mustang escorts. Determined to hunt down the enemy air units, the AAF directed P-51 squadrons to begin flying alternate escorts and low-level fighter sweeps. As strafing missions began, the loss of Mustangs increased. Many small caliber AA guns ringed Japanese airfields and the liquid-cooled Merlin engine of the P-51 was vulnerable to damage that would cause any loss of coolant.

However, the worst enemy of the Mustangs was weather. Towering fronts encountered between Iwo Jima and Japan had forced the return of some missions. The one of 26 June 1945 was an exception. Led by B-29s as navigators, all three P-51 groups plunged into a severe weather complex en route to Honshu. Twenty-seven Mustangs and 25 pilots were lost.

Despite the multiple perils of the VLR missions, joint AAF-Navy planning had established a remarkable Air Sea Rescue (ASR) system that saved hundreds of B-29 and P-51 crews. Rescue units were positioned all the way from Iwo Jima to just off the coast of Honshu. The rescue operation included U.S. Navy submarines (known as the Lifeguard League) and destroyer-escorts stationed at specific map references. ASR aircraft included B-29s patrolling offshore, both Navy and AAF Catalinas, B-17 Flying Fortresses with life boats, and Navy Privateers. P-61 night fighters also located strays with radar and accompanied them back to base. These efforts paid off as dozens of airmen were plucked from the ocean.

Iwo Jima's Mustangs achieved their primary goal of driving Japanese fighters from the defense of Honshu. After May 1945 B-29 losses to Japanese fighters were extremely rare. The second goal, the total destruction of Japanese air power, was thwarted only by the enemy's deceptive efforts. They avoided combat in most cases, husbanding their remaining air units for the expected invasion. But in the end, the Allies enjoyed virtual air supremacy over the Empire.

Iwo Jima from 10,000 feet. Mount Suribachi is south, at the bottom of the photo, and the airfields can be seen toward the center and north coast. (Author's Collection)

Right: The ground echelon of the 15th Fighter Group went ashore on Iwo Jima just two weeks after the invasion. With the ground campaign still in full fury, they burrowed into the volcanic ash, built bunkers of sand bags and scraps of lumber, and lived like moles. (USAF)

Left: A Japanese mortar round destroyed the 78th Squadron's command post. (Author's Collection)

Right: Along with the litter of battle, 15th Fighter Group personnel found this unexploded 16 inch shell from a U.S. Navy battleship. (Author's Collection)

The U.S. military "horn of plenty" was overflowing by 1945. Aircraft carriers were so numerous that CVEs, like *Marcus Island* CVE-77, were employed in the continuous task of ferrying replacement aircraft. Here a deck load of factory-fresh North American P-51D-25 Mustangs are en route to Pacific bases. (NARS)

When the 15th Fighter Group arrived on Saipan with its new mounts to participate in the final air campaign against Japan, older AAF fighters were destined for the scrap heap. A new P-51 Mustang (right) takes a nostalgic flight with a pair of 318th Fighter Group veterans, a P-38 Lightning (center) and a razorback P-47D Thunderbolt (left). (NARS)

8 March 1945, the 15th Fighter Group (45th, 47th, and 78th Squadrons) assembles over Saipan en route to its future base of operations on Iwo Jima. This was the beginning of the AAF's buildup of fighter forces on Iwo. The P-51D in the upper left corner is that of group CO, Colonel James Beckwith. (USAF)

Above: Colonel Jim Beckwith (in cockpit) and his charges immediately began close support of the Marines on Iwo Jima and pounded nearby islands of the Bonin Group. (Author's Collection)

Below: The Iwo strikes were short hops with a 500-pounder under each wing. (Jim VanderHey)

Northrop P-61 Black Widows of the 6th and 548th Night Fighter Squadrons arrived on Iwo Jima early in March to protect against Japanese raiders. Utilizing their radar, they also assisted in locating stray Mustangs and flew harassment sorties to the Bonin Islands. This is the flight line of the 548th. (USAF)

The crew of MIDNIGHT MICKEY, 6th Night Fighter Squadron, claimed one Betty destroyed and one probable on the night of 25 March 1945 near Iwo Jima: (l. to r.) radar operator, Dan Hinz; pilot, Myrle McCumber; and observer, Pete Dutkanicz. This same crew had previously downed a raider near Saipan. (E.R. Thomas)

Above: Sagging tents of the 21st Fighter Group, (46th, 72nd, and 531st Squadrons) perforated by bullet holes and grenade fragments, are seen on the morning after the predawn Banzai attack of 26 March 1945. The bodies of several Japanese soldiers lie in the foreground. (USAF)

Left: Pilots of the 21st Fighter Group remove the body of a dead comrade. Some Japanese wielded sabres. (Author's Collection)

These 21st Fighter Group pilots had yet to fly a combat mission over Japan when they fought a ground battle on Iwo Jima on 26 March 1945. All survived the subsequent air campaign over Japan.

Captain Ray Kessler, a veteran of the Marshall's campaign, collected a Japanese sword after the ground battle. (USAF)

Lieutenant Joe Coons compares American (left) and Japanese grenades. Coons later scored one and one-half victories over Honshu. (USAF)

Lieutenant Paul Wine received a minor wound as he played dead in a Japanese bunker. Wine later scored a kill and a probable over Japan. (USAF)

Lieutenant George Metcalf admires his trophy sword from the battlefield. Metcalf later scored one aerial victory over Japan. (USAF)

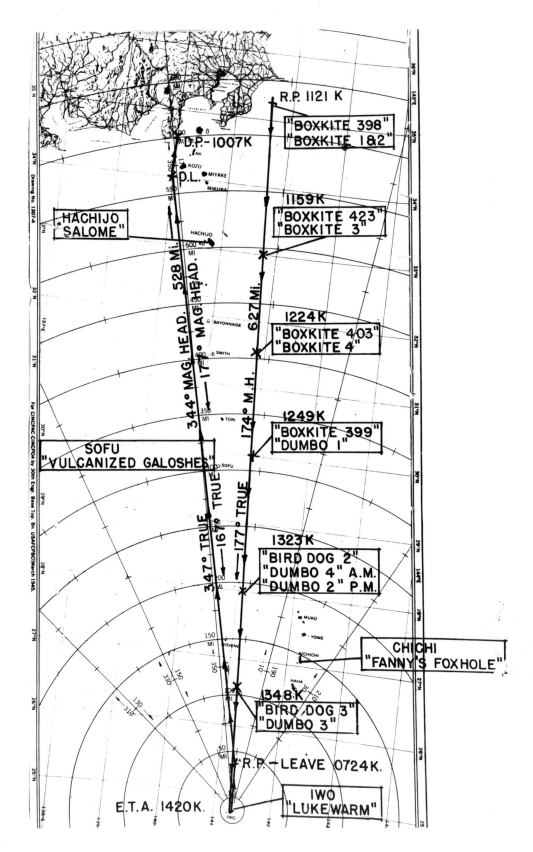

Fighter pilots flying from Iwo Jima to the Empire were provided with strip maps for each mission to assist in navigation over the open ocean. A reduced version is reproduced here. This map shows the northbound route to Tokyo Bay and the return from a point offshore noted as R.P., the Rally Point. Code names were used for everything in order to foil Japanese listening stations that might intercept radio transmissions. Landmarks and rescue units were all given names that the Japanese were not likely to identify with. Iwo Jima was "Lukewarm," Chichi Jima had the bawdy title of "Fanny's Foxhole," etc. Various air or sea rescue units stationed along the return route were labeled "Bird Dog," "Dumbo," or "Boxkite." With each mission these elaborate procedures were recreated. (Author's Collection)

Above: Captain Robert W. Moore, 78th Squadron, looks apprehensive as he awaits takeoff orders on 7 April 1945 for the first VLR mission from Iwo Jima to Honshu. A 110-gallon drop tank hangs on sway braces under each wing. He destroyed a pair of Mitsubishi A6M Hamps. (Robert W. Moore)

Below: Just back from Tokyo, Major (later Brigadier General) Jim VandeHey, CO of the 78th Squadron, sits on the wing and relates details of the historic mission to pilots and ground crews. VandeHey scored a victory over a Ki-46 Dinah that got too close to the B-29s. (James VandeHey)

Major Jim Tapp (later Colonel), who rose to command of the 78th Squadron, 15th Fighter Group, downed eight Japanese aircraft over Honshu, four while defending B-29s on the first VLR mission, 7 April 1945. (Author's Collection)

Majors Harry Crim (left) and DeWitt Spain (right), 21st Fighter Group, brief Brigadier General Mickey Moore, Seventh Fighter Command CO, on the 7 April 1945 air battle over Tokyo. Crim, leading the 531st Squadron, shot down a Nick and a Tony. (USAF)

Left: 1st Lieutenant Robert G. Anderson, 531st Squadron, 21st Fighter Group, was the only loss on the 7 April 1945 mission to Tokyo. He was killed when his Mustang crashed northeast of Tokyo. (Yoji Watanabe)

Safety be damned! When a mission to the Empire departed or returned, everyone assembled and lined the runway. It was 12 April 1945 and the spectators were from the 21st Fighter Group. (USAF)

Captain Francis Ennis (left) and 2nd Lieutenant Alvan Roberts combined to share a 45th Squadron victory over Japan on 12 April 1945. The enemy aircraft was a Nick. (USAF)

Parachuting from Mustangs of the Seventh Fighter Command caused several early fatalities. A practice sling was rigged so that pilots could get a feel for the problem. However, most of the dead were believed to have struck the tail as they left the cockpit. (Author's Collection)

Above: North American P-51D Mustangs of the 46th Squadron, 21st Fighter Group, taxi into position for a mission to Honshu carrying 110-gallon wing tanks. (USAF)

Below: A flight of 45th Squadron, 15th Fighter Group, Mustangs en route to the Empire. (USAF)

Above: A battle-damaged B-29 of the 504th Bomb Group landed on Iwo lacking hydraulics and crashed into a line of parked 45th Fighter Squadron Mustangs. The crew of the B-29 survived, and there were no casualties among the fighter community. Exploding ammunition sent rescuers scurrying. (Author's Collection)

Right: Captain Jim Van Nada, badly wounded in the 26 March 1945 ground battle, was evacuated to Hawaii. He could have gone home, but the Marshalls' veteran returned to Iwo Jima and took command of the 72nd Squadron. He had scored a rare victory over Mili and claimed another over Yokohama. (Jim Van Nada)

Above: A pair of 46th Squadron, 21st Fighter Group P-51s returning from Honshu. (Author's Collection)

Below: Iwo Jima-based fighter pilots, almost crippled from confinement in their cockpits after the six to eight hour Empire missions, were given the luxury of a hot tub (including cold beer) and a rub down. Navy construction battalions built the facility, Iwo's sulfur springs provided the hot water. (Morgan Redwine)

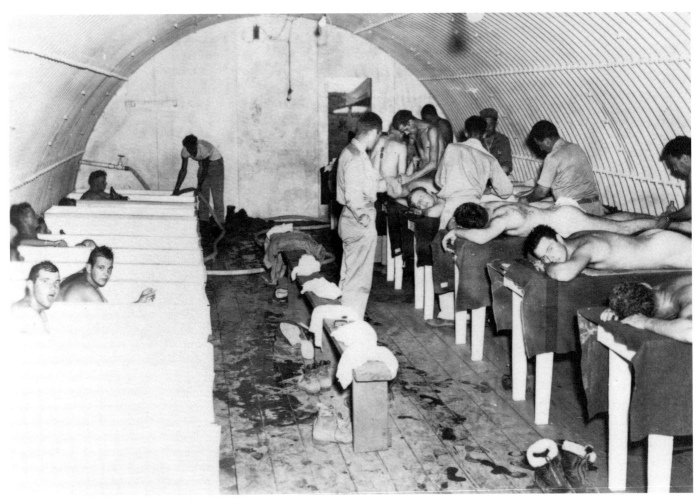

On 12 April 1945 1st Lieutenant Robert Campbell, 46th Squadron, 21st Fighter Group, returned from Tokyo despite an encounter with Japanese fighters that scored a hit on the canopy directly over his head. He was miraculously unhurt. His squadron downed five Japanese fighters. (USAF)

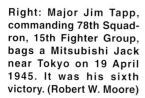

Right: Major Jim Tapp, commanding 78th Squadron, 15th Fighter Group, bags a Mitsubishi Jack near Tokyo on 19 April 1945. It was his sixth victory. (Robert W. Moore)

Left: Lieutenant Don Statsmann, 45th Squadron, 15th Fighter Group, flames a Mitsubishi J2M Jack over Honshu on 19 April 1945. (Don Statsmann)

Right: Major Robert Moore, 15th Fighter Group hits and downs a Nakajima Ki-43 Oscar low over Akenogahara airdrome on 22 April 1945. (Author's Collection)

Left: A Nakajima Ki-115 Tsurugi (sword), developed as a low cost suicide aircraft, gets itself in the gun sight of Major Robert Moore on 30 April. He registered many hits but did not see the Japanese plane crash, so claimed a probable. However, their could be no happy outcome for the Japanese pilot. The plane was designed to either crash against an opponent or at best crash land. Once it was airborne, the wheels dropped off. (Author's Collection)

A pair of 78th Squadron, 15th Fighter Group Mustangs are readied for a VLR mission.

Above: WEE LONA LEE is preflighted. The snake's head insignia stems from the squadron's Panama service in the 1930s. (Jim VandeHey)

Below: Captain Vic Mollan (left) watches as sway braces are attached to a 110 gallon wing tank. (Jim VandeHey)

Loss of power on takeoff was a frequent menace for Iwo Jima based fighters. Condensation in fuel tanks or engine failure due to any number of mechanical problems was nearly always disastrous for aircraft that were heavily loaded with fuel and ammunition.

Above: A 21st Fighter Group P-51 lifts off over the wreckage of 2nd Lieutenant Claude A. Lane's 72nd Squadron Mustang. Crash crews helped a badly shaken Lane from the cockpit, then fought the fire. (USAF)

Below: 1st Lieutenant Tom Quinn, 46th Squadron, had better luck with LITTLE ANGEL. Its fuel did not ignite. (USAF)

Above: This 531st Squadron Mustang also went off the end of the runway with engine failure. The pilot walked away, but JEANETTE was only good for spare parts. (USAF)

Below: Iwo's gritty dust was highly corrosive, requiring frequent engine changes. Such a replacement involved extensive manhandling. This is a 15th Fighter Group crew. (USAF)

Left: Colonel Ken Powell, CO of the 21st Fighter Group was wounded in the Banzai attack of 26 March 1945. He was relieved by a Seventh Air Force veteran who had led the 72nd Squadron at Makin, Colonel Charles Taylor, shown here by his Mustang. Taylor's P-51 was disabled by flak on 25 May 1945, and he parachuted successfully near a lifeguard submarine. (Author's Collection)

Below: Mustangs of the 21st Fighter Group assembled on Iwo Jima. Markings show the 72nd Squadron on the right, the the 46th Squadron in the background, and the 531st Squadron nearest the camera. Visible serial numbers are all for P-51D-20-NA models. (USAF)

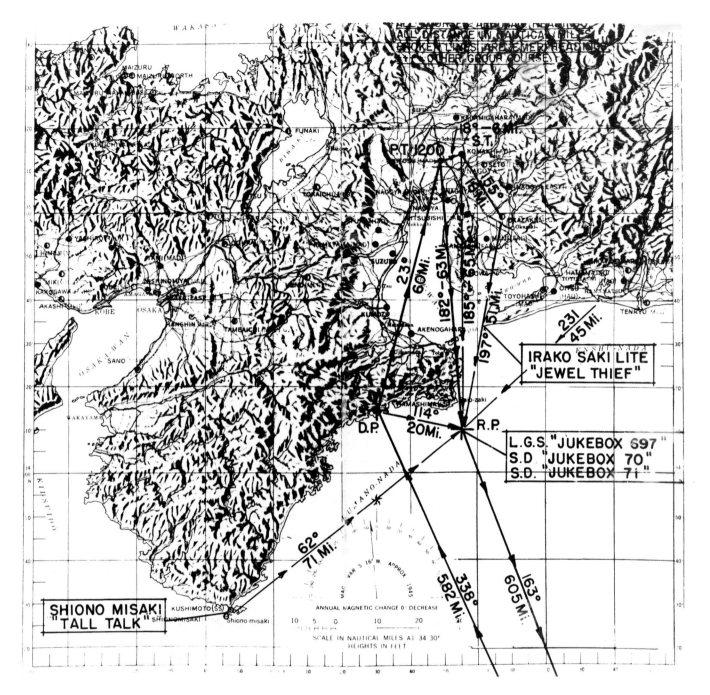

A target map for a Seventh Fighter Command sweep of Komaki AD, north of Nagoya provides Mustang pilots with essential information including distances and magnetic headings of approach and departure routes. Major shoreline landmarks, Shiono Misaki point and Irako Saki light house, were given snappy code names, as were rescue units. Jukebox 697 was a submarine of the Life Guard League, the other two Jukebox references are for aircraft. The R.P. is the rally point at which a B-29 navigator and rescue craft would wait. Osaka, another major city frequently visited by AAF forces, lies just to the west. (Author's Collection)

A Boeing B-29 navigates toward the Japanese Empire with Mustangs of the 15th Fighter Group's 45th Squadron. Even on a bomber escort mission, the fighters would fly their own route, rendezvousing with the bombers off the coast of Japan. (USAF)

Left: Major Robert Moore, 78th Squadron, destroys a Zeke north of Matsudo Airdrome on 25 May 1945. The small blur to the right is the pilot who has just jumped from the stricken aircraft. This was Moore's second Zeke victory on this mission during which the 15th Fighter Group claimed eight. (Author's Collection)

Right: Returning from a 25 May 1945 strafing mission to Matsudo Airdrome outside Tokyo, 1st Lieutenant Walter Kreimann, 78th Squadron, 15th Fighter Group, was just two hours from home when his engine temperature suddenly rose and flames began to lick back from the engine. He cracked the canopy and rolled the plane over but was stuck momentarily with fire in his face. Kicking loose, he descended to the seemingly empty ocean. His mates had summoned a lifeguard submarine, and with help from an orbiting B-29, the U.S.S. *Tigrone* effected a rescue. Kreimann is seen here in his raft alongside the sub. His face shows the burns sustained before getting free from his Mustang. (USN)

The lifeguard submarine *Trepang* took the prize for rescuing downed airmen. She is seen here late in June 1945 in Guam harbor with twenty-eight B-29 crew members and a pair of fighter pilots. It was the second P-51 bail-out for Captain Frank Ayers (standing, center in sun tans), a record, and one that caused him to be returned home. Ayers and 2nd Lieutenant Lamar Christian (far right, arm in sling) were both from the 47th Fighter Squadron. (USN)

Lieutenant Colonel Julian "Jack" Thomas, had led a squadron in the Marshall Islands. He assumed command of the 15th Fighter Group in May 1945. Considered a daring but reckless flyer, he was killed in action when the wings of his P-51 buckled during a dive over Kagamigahara Airdrome, Nagoya on 19 July 1945. (Author's Collection)

Colonel John Mitchell, who had led the 1943 Solomons mission to get Admiral Yamamoto, returned to the Pacific in 1945 and joined the Seventh Fighter Command. He succeeded Jack Thomas as CO of the 15th Fighter Group. Mitchell scored three kills over Japan raising his total to eleven victories. (Author's Collection)

The 506th Fighter Group, the third and last Mustang unit to operate from Iwo, musters for a mission to Japan.

Above: As a 458th Squadron pilot awaits the signal to start engines and taxi, his crew chief stands on the wing to render any final assistance. In order to conserve fuel, engines were not turned over until the last minute. (NARS)

Below: The 506th Group begins taking off in pairs. Dust from departing P-51s often made successive takeoffs hazardous. (USAF)

The North American P-51 was not originally intended as a low-level attack aircraft. One bullet in its coolant system caused the engine to become inoperative within a short time. However, as the Japanese air forces avoided combat, airfield strafing missions became more frequent than B-29 escort missions. Except for the coolant weakness, the Mustang could absorb considerable structural damage and return its pilots.

Above: 1st Lieutenant Bob Beyl took a cannon round that shattered his canopy, holed the fuselage, and loosened a panel. (Author's Collection)

Left and below: 1st Lieutenant Tom McCullough's aircraft, was hit from behind by a bullet that ricocheted off the armor plate and blew a football-size hole in the canopy. Both pilots were with the 78th Squadron, 15th Fighter Group. (Louis Korb)

1st Lieutenant Eldon Westlund, 78th Squadron, 15th Fighter Group, was barely clearing protective bunkers at Akenogahara Airdrome, south of Nagoya (above left) when he shot these pictures with his Mustang's gun camera. He was credited with the destruction of one Nakajima Tojo (above right). (Les Twigg)

Lieutenant Don Gordon, and the 21st Fighter Group found a few targets parked in the open on Kisarazu Airdrome on the eastern shore of Tokyo Bay during an 8 May 1945 sweep: a Mitsubishi G3M Nell (foreground), a Nakajima C6N Myrt (left), and a Nakajima J1N1 Irving (center), next to a pair of Mitsubishi G4M Bettys. (Author's Collection)

Escort and airfield strafing were the primary mission of Iwo Jima-based fighters. Secondary targets of opportunity, included transportation. Here Mustangs strafe rail lines near Toba, blowing the boiler of a locomotive. (Author's Collection)

Lieutenant Leon Sher, 47th Squadron, 15th Fighter Group, strafed an anchored Japanese escort vessel, CD 30 in Sagami Bay on 8 June 1945. Rounds from his six .50 caliber machine guns can be seen where they hit the water and then the vessel. Some of the Mustangs fire touched off an explosion in the ready magazine. The ship was grounded to save it from sinking. (Leon Sher)

Above: MARGARET IV gets a load of rockets and the big 165-gallon tanks for a mission to the Empire. This was Major Jim Tapp's P-51. He was CO of the 78th Squadron, 15th Fighter Group. Only one squadron in each group was assigned as rocket carriers. (Author's Collection)

Below: Tapp inspects the five-inch rockets mounted under each wing next to the extra large auxiliary tank. The rockets were highly destructive if they could be placed on a suitable target. But few pilots appreciated the added weight and drag for the 700 mile trip. (Louis Korb)

A new radio directional device was utilized on all Iwo Jima-based Mustangs. It received the Morse code signals U and D transmitted from Iwo Jima and was affectionately know as "Uncle Dog".

Above: Tech Sergeant Charles Barr fashioned a link trainer from a165-gallon drop tank to familiarize pilots with the directional unit. (Charles Barr)

Below: The homing unit's twin aerials are seen on the fuselage behind the canopy on this 506th Fighter Group P-51. (Jim Hinkle)

No. 640, SHAWNEE PRINCESS was a P-51D-20NA, 462nd Squadron, 506th Fighter Group. It went down after engine failure following a mission to Chichi Jima. Pilot Ed Serle was rescued. (Author's Collection)

Mustangs of the 506th Fighter Group nestle in close to the right waist window of a B-29. The P-51 pilots relied on Superfortress crews to help them with the long over-water navigation to and from the Empire, and the bomber crews depended on the Mustangs for protection. (USAF)

Left: A battle damaged B-29, a dead pilot at the controls, arrived over Iwo Jima without hydraulics and the crew was ordered to parachute rather than risk a crash landing. The Superfort with its dead pilot continued on, then made a gentle turn back toward Iwo. A 548th Night Fighter Squadron Black Widow was directed to down the "Flying Dutchman." Seen here is the crew of that P-61: (l. to r.) pilot, Lieutenant Art Sheperd; radar operator, Lieutenant Arvid Shulenberger; and observer, Master Sergeant Donald Meech. When the 548th transferred to Ie Shima, they scored the squadron's first victory over Japanese night attackers. (Author's Collection)

Pilots of the 457th Squadron, 506th Fighter Group pose before a P-51D. (l. to r.) Top Row: John Hugo, Curtis Worthen and Bill Hutchinson. Kneeling: Evelyn Neff, John Benbow, and Tom Messall. Neff and Benbow were both killed over Honshu. In the air campaign from Iwo Jima 116 air crew members were lost to all operational causes; flak, fighters, accidents, and weather. (Dr. John Benbow)

With the vast expanse of ocean between Honshu and Iwo Jima, the air-sea rescue system had to be highly organized and sophisticated.

Above: Some of the equipment utilized by the AAF's 4th Emergency Rescue Squadron was the OA-10 (right), an AAF version of the Catalina PBY-5A flying boat, and a specially equipped Boeing B-17. They were known, respectively, as "Dumbo" and "Super Dumbo". (Author's Collection)

Right: The B-17 lugged a motor launch under its belly, to be parachuted to downed airmen. The white blister just under the nose housed search radar. (Raymond Cole)

Below: Flying from Iwo Jima, VPB-121 Privateers engaged in armed reconnaissance missions and provided plane guard duty for rescue submarines off the coast of Honshu. AC of TAIL CHASER was Lt. Norman Ebel. Back row (l. to r.) Bob Duncan, Mike Runnels, John Hardison, Francis Henderson, Forrest Perry, and Bob Fagala. Front row (l. to r.) Louis Busch, Stan Holiday, Lt. Ebel, James Risley, and Paul McGuire. (John Ebel)

Lieutenant Yutaka Morioka flew a Mitsubishi Zeke from Atsugi with the 321st Kokutai. He lost his right hand to the tail guns of a B-29 but survived to continue flying. He was fitted with a hook on the left arm to handle throttle controls. (Author's Collection)

In a 3 August 1945 dogfight near Tokyo Bay, Morioka attacked a flight of Mustangs providing cover for a rescue operation. He shot down 2nd Lieutenant John Coneff who was flying a P-51 of the 457th Fighter Squadron. (Author's Collection)

Captain Ed Mikes, 458th Squadron, the subject of the massive rescue operation after he parachuted, is seen here on the submarine, *Aspro*, after being retrieved from a B-17's motor launch. (NARS)

On 3 August 1945 a 506th Fighter Group P-51 pilot, Capt. Ed Mikes, was hit by flak near Tokyo and went down in Sagami Bay triggering a monumental rescue attempt. A B-17 Super Dumbo dropped a motor boat near Mikes and summoned a rescue submarine. While Mustangs orbited, submarine *Aspro* proceeded toward a rescue rendezvous.

Top Right: Japanese Zekes and then a pair of Petes (one seen at far left) attempted to interfere, boldly taking on a pair of VPB-121 Privateers (one is at far right) that had set up a CAP over the rescue operation. (John Ebel)

Center Right: Both Mitsubishi F1M Petes were downed by the PB4Y-2s assemblage of gun turrets, and this one was photographed from Lt. Cdr. R.J. Pflum's aircraft as it flamed into the bay. (John Ebel)

Below: Lt. Cdr. R. J. Pflum commanded VPB-121 based on Iwo Jima. LOTTA TAYLE, with co-pilot Lt. (jg) Cormac Malloy seen here, was Pflum's Privateer. (John Ebel)

The Kawasaki Ki-61 Tony was a beautifully sleek Japanese fighter but was plagued with an unreliable liquid-cooled power plant. Late in the war the airframe was modified to accept a Mitsubishi radial engine which improved performance substantially. Redesignated the Ki-100, insufficient numbers were produced to have any impact on the outcome of the war. This line of Ki-100s is from the 1st Chutai, 59th Sentai serving on Home Island defense. (Ernie McDowell)

A P-51D-20 Mustang of the 46th Squadron, 21st Fighter Group, loaded with 110 gallon auxiliary wing tanks, awaits takeoff orders on Airfield No. 2. The pilot is in the cockpit and the crew chief hovers on the wing. Mount Suribachi, the scene of the historic Marine flag-raising, is in the background. (USAF)

Captain Jack Ort (above) and 1st Lieutenant Marcus McDilda (below) were strafing Hanshin Airdrome near Osaka on 8 August 1945 when their 46th Squadron Mustangs were disabled by Japanese AA and both were imprisoned. Taken to Japanese secret police headquarters, they were interrogated separately regarding their knowledge of the A-bomb that had been dropped on Hiroshima. Ort was apparently uncooperative and was executed by a furious Japanese officer. McDilda who knew nothing of the Hiroshima attack, but had been told about the process of nuclear fission by a squadronmate, explained what little he knew of the scientific wonder. McDilda lived to be sent to a POW camp. Ort's executioner was found, tried and hung by a War Crimes Trial. (Author's Collection)

93

The last AAF fighter unit to arrive in the Pacific was the 414th Fighter Group. Commanded by Colonel (later Lieutenant General) Henry Thorne, a Philippine veteran, the P-47N-equipped group flew a practice mission to Truk (losing one pilot to AA fire) before moving on to Iwo Jima in July 1945. They flew just three VLR missions before VJ-day and scored only one aerial victory. (Ernie McDowell)

A P-47N of the 456th Squadron crashed short of Iwo's North Field, killing the pilot, 2nd Lieutenant Walter Cecot. (USAF)

Major Robert W. Moore recorded 12 aerial victories, one in the Marshalls and eleven over Japan. He flew with both the 78th and 45th Squadrons of the 15th Fighter Group, and became CO of the 45th. (USAF)

Major Harry Crim was CO, 531st Squadron and scored six victories over Japan. His No. 300 is seen with CC, Staff Sergeant Lee Siciliano in the cockpit. (Author's Collection)

On this and the succeeding three pages is a gallery of Iwo Jima based fighters, pilots, and ground crews.

This well traveled P-51D-25 was flown by several pilots including Colonel John Mitchell, last CO of the 15th Fighter Group, and bore their accumulated score and mission marks: five aerial kills, three aircraft destroyed on the ground in 28 missions. (Author's Collection)

Captain Walter Powell (left) and Lieutenant Joe Brunette stand by HAIRLESS JOE, a 47th Squadron P-51. Powell was killed in action on 30 July 1945. (Author's Collection)

Capt. Eurich Bright, 47th Squadron, 15th Fighter Group scored three and one-half kills over Japan. (Author's Collection)

Right: The Mustangs of the 47th Squadron, 15th Fighter Group were adorned with characters from the Al Capp comic strip, Lil' Abner, artfully recreated by Staff Sergeant James Lindsay. (Author's Collection)

2nd Lieutenant Lester Twigg. (Author's Collection)

The name, APPASIONATTA VAN CLIMAX, required the long nose of the P-51. (Hank Weinberger)

1st Lieutenant John Fitzgerald (right) and crew chief, Sergeant Gillard Andrews. (John Fitzgerald)

1st Lieutenant Hayden Sparks (right) and crew chief, Staff Sergeant Bill Crossin. Sparks was Thomas's wingman when the latter was killed. (Author's Collection)

1st Lieutenant Bob Louwers (left) and S/Sgt. John Lakovic, CC, 46th Squadron (Bob Louwers)

Major Fred Shirley, CO, 46th Squadron. He claimed four victories. (Bob Louwers)

1st Lieutenant Robert Campbell, 46th Squadron. (Bob Louwers)

1st Lieutenant Ted Perritt, 72nd Squadron. (Manly Fouts)

1st Lieutenant John Brock (left) and Major Robert Mc Donald, 46th Squadron. SLOW ROLL was Brock's P-51 in which he scored three kills. (Author's Collection)

1st Lieutenant Charles O. Rainwater, 46th Squadron, scored kills over a Jack, Tojo, and a Tony. (USAF)

Right: BAKERSFIELD
BARONESS, a P-51 of the
458th Squadron, shows
the unit's distinctive
candy stripe tail.
(Author's Collection)

Left: KWITCHERBITCHIN,
was a 457th Squadron
Mustang. The Squadron
had red tails. (Author's
Collection)

Right: Lieutenant Ed
Balhorn, 462nd Squadron
in the yellow-tailed P-51,
MEATBALL. The mission
symbols reflect escort
and fighter sweeps. The
rearing stallion insignia
was on all 462nd
Mustangs. (Author's
Collection)

Left: Lieutenant Morgan Redwine, 46th Squadron, 21st Fighter Group and LIL' EVIE. (Morgan Redwine)

Below: The Republic P-47N Thunderbolt equipped the 414th Fighter Group's three squadrons, the 413th, 437th, and 456th. Shown here is a blue-tailed N of the 456th with the ultimate — 300 gallon — external fuel tanks, giving it a range of 800 miles. (Author's Collection)

Left: HUEY, a yellow-tailed Thunderbolt of the 413th Squadron, 414th Fighter Group, rests next to a checker-tailed P-47N of the 437th Squadron. (George Lovering)

4

FINAL BLOWS BY TASK FORCE 38

Through May 1945 the bulk of the Pacific fleet hovered between Okinawa and Kyushu, lending support to the former by battering Japanese bases on the latter. Task Force 58, comprising the fast carriers, was continuously engaged with Japanese raiders bound for Okinawa or intent on striking the fleet itself. Of particular interest to Japanese attackers were the large aircraft carriers.

On 4-5 May 1945 the Royal Navy carriers, *Formidable, Indomitable,* and *Victorious* were all crashed by Kamikazes, but continued on station. When *Formidable* was hit a second time her air wing was so depleted that she had to retire. To the north, *Bunker Hill* was also hit on 4 May, damaged so seriously that she limped back to Bremerton, Washington. *Enterprise,* the grand old lady of the Pacific fleet, was knocked out of the war by a Kamikaze but survived. Both ships suffered heavy casualties.

Task Force 58 withdrew and was replaced in June 1945 by Task Force 38 which ultimately fielded sixteen fast carriers. Its main effort from 10 June onward was conducted in Japanese home waters against airfield and naval targets. The Japanese Imperial Fleet had been masters of the Pacific in December 1941. Now its remnants were hounded and sunk at their moorings without again sailing to the defense of the Empire. Ranging from the northern island of Hokkaido to Kyushu with carrier strikes, Task Force 38 warships even shelled coastal cities with impunity. Only Japanese air units contested their passage.

When a final post war tally was taken, only one Japanese battleship, four carriers, 15 light cruisers and 27 destroyers remained afloat in various ports.

More Marine squadrons flying F4Us joined the Pacific air war in May 1945. A VMF-512 Corsair is seen here in the catapult sling, throttle up, on *Gilbert Islands* CVE-107 (USN)

The veteran aircraft carrier *Essex* took her last air group aboard in March 1945, and entered combat in April.

Above: A Curtiss Helldiver of VB-83 unfolds its wings prior to launching. (MNA)

Below: An F6F-5 Hellcat of VF-83 in flight. The words on the fuselage are: DEATH & DESTRUCTION. This may have been the Hellcat of Lieutenant Tad Coleman, Jr. who eventually scored 10 victories. His first two were claimed while flying with VF-6 in late 1943 and early 1944. (MNA)

Armorers load .50 caliber ammunition on an F6F-5 of VF-83 aboard *Essex.* The wings are folded. (USN)

During operations over the Ryukyus, *Yorktown* VT-9 Avengers collided in mid-air. Lieutenant (jg) W. Patterson (left) and his crew members, Eral Ellis and McArdle landed safely despite the absence of most of the right horizontal stabilizer (MNA)

Above: Lieutenant (jg) Bill Cromley simulates flying an Avenger at night. VT(N)-90 was part of Night Air Group 90 operating off *Enterprise*. They not only provided night air protection for the fleet, but conducted offensive night missions with their radar equipped aircraft. (Author's Collection)

Below: A VT(N)-90 TBM-3D landed long and crashed into parked aircraft doing considerable damage. (Bill Balden)

On 14 May 1945, off Kyushu, the Japanese finally succeeded in knocking out *Enterprise* CV-6. Over 24 Zekes approached the Enterprise. The combat air patrol downed 19 and AA accounted for six. However, a single Kamikaze pilot carrying a 550 pound bomb under his Zeke, dove into the flight deck, setting off an explosion that blew the #1 elevator 400 feet in the air. The gaping hole seen here is the former location of the elevator. The gallant crew brought the fires under control, but damage was so severe that the ship could neither launch nor recover aircraft. Personnel losses were 14 dead and 68 wounded. The "Big E" departed for Ulithi and then the U.S. after nearly three and one-half years in the Pacific war. It was the third time a Japanese aircraft crashed the ship. (USN)

Above: On 15 July 1945 Task Force 38 launched strikes against the northernmost Japanese island of Hokkaido. Heavy clouds prevented low level attack at some targets, so the Navy carrier aircraft conducted an unusual level-bombing of facilities at Hakodate. Seen here are VB-83 Helldivers (left) and VT-83 Avengers (right) from *Essex*. The lead TBM-3E (foreground) has an AN/APS-4 radar pod installed under the right wing. The squadron leader used his radar to identify and bomb ground targets. Others in the formation salvoed their bombs when the leader dropped. (MNA)

Below: Parts of Nemuru, Hokkaido burn furiously after the carrier strike. (USN)

Above: The last *Essex* class fast carrier to join the Pacific Fleet was *Shangri-La* CV-38 early in 1945, bringing Air Group 85 to the battle. She is seen here with F4U-1C and dash D aircraft on deck, a *Craven* class destroyer abreast. The C model Corsairs (#41 center) were armed with a pair of 20 mm cannons in each wing. The carrier's name was derived from a mythical lost kingdom in Tibet, featured in the 1937 movie, "Lost Horizon." After the 1942 Doolittle raid on Tokyo, President Franklin Roosevelt was asked by puzzled newsmen where the raiders had come from. To protect the secret naval operation the president responded, "Shangri-La." (Bob Ketenheim)

Below: These Grumman F6F-5Ps, the photo recon version of the Hellcat, were from Air Group 85, unlike many photo aircraft, the Hellcats retained their armament. The drop tanks are the 150 gallon variety. (NARS via Bob Ketenheim)

Kure Naval Base, at the southern tip of Honshu was under frequent air attack by both AAF B-24s and U.S. Navy carrier aircraft from mid-March 1945 to the end of July. On 24-28 July a series of strikes by Task Force 38 damaged repair and logistic facilities and major warships at anchor. In the bay near the top center of the photo, BB *Ise*, is hit repeatedly while at her moorings, as seen by *Hancock's* Air Group 6. Approximately 17 bomb hits put her on the bottom. Note the Avenger in flight, right center. (MNA)

The heavy cruiser *Tone*, shown here under attack in Etauchi Bay, Eta Jima Island, was badly battered by Navy bombers on 24 July 1945 but remained afloat. Hit by another carrier strike on 28 July she was flooded. The anchored vessels were not helpless. They fought back with their AA batteries downing many attackers. This photo was taken by an Air Group 85 aircraft from *Shangri-La*. VB-87 from *Ticonderoga* lost eight of 13 Helldivers bombing battleship *Hyuga*. (MNA)

Above: Battleship *Haruna*, tucked into a bay close to the shore of Eta Jima Island, near Kure, is taken under attack by Task Force 38 aircraft. This veteran of Pacific sea battles had suffered slight damage in earlier air attacks, but she was finally sunk at her moorings under a rain of bombs on 28 July 1945. (USN)

Below: Strike units from Task Force 38 hit Nagoya and Kobe in central Honshu on 30 July 1945 during a shipping hunt. Air Group 6 from *Hancock* was part of this attack. VT-6 Avengers were closely escorted by VBF-6 Corsairs (in the distance above), but shortly after this photo was taken the TBM-3E in the center foreground was hit by Japanese AA fire. Pilot, Ensign Cliff Bausor, and his two crewmen, John Streeter and John Vehan, were killed. (MNA)

Above: A Fairey Firefly with battle damage to its right wing makes it back to H.M.S. *Indefatigable*, in July 1945. The pilot is Sub Lieutenant J. MacLaren of 1772 Squadron (Jerry Scutts)

Below: A Royal Navy Corsair, looking for a temporary home, landed on *Shangri -La*. (NARS via Bob Ketenheim)

Above: A Curtiss Helldiver launched from *Makassar Strait* CVE-91 dips dangerously close to the water just over the bow. (USN)

Below: The pilot finally gained air speed and altitude, leaving a wake on the water as he averted disaster. The CVE was replenishing squadrons of Task Force 38 fast carriers in August 1945 (USN)

Above: A late model Curtiss SB2C-4E of VB-85 from *Shangri-La* in August 1945. The pilot is Ensign M.L. Skinner and the gunner is E.T. Tuohey. (NARS via Bob Ketenheim)

Below: A neat formation of Curtiss SB2C-4E Helldivers of VB-87 from *Ticonderoga* CV-14 in August 1945. This version of the Helldiver had 20mm cannons instead of .50 caliber machine guns. (USN)

The end of the war was just three days away, and a pair of VPB-121 Privateers were patrolling off the coast of Honshu near Tokyo Bay. Their mission was to scout for any Japanese warships that might venture out to intercept Task Force 38 and to render assistance to downed aviators. The patrol was jumped from above by six Zekes.

Above: Lieutenant Commander John Rainey's "Y495" was shot down, and four of the crew were killed, the others surviving a crash landing for brief imprisonment. Lieutenant Tom Allen's plane was badly damaged, but he returned it to Iwo Jima on three engines. It was the last air-to-air engagement of the war for the multi-engine patrol bombers. (Karl Gaber via John Ebel)

Below: The crew of Y495. Back row (l. to r.) Karl Gaber, Carl Bremer (KIA), Robert Guth (KIA), J. Frasburc, Richard Cox, and Arthur Dugger. Front row (l. to r.) Delman Mott (KIA), Harold Whitted, Rainey, Edward Heeb (KIA), and William Long. (Karl Gaber via John Ebel)

Above: A Corsair of VBF-85 makes a successful one gear crash landing on *Shangri-La.* CV-38 had a squadron each of F4U fighters and fighter-bombers, a common mix in 1945. VBF-85 scored the last Corsair victory of the war when Ensign Falvey Sandidge, Jr., flying CAP, downed a Judy as it approached the fleet off Honshu on 15 August. (NARS via Bob Ketenheim)

Right: At 1400 on 15 August 1945, Ensign Clarence A. "Bill" Moore, of VF-31 from *Belleau Wood,* intercepted and shot down a Yokosuka D4Y Judy approaching the fleet off Honshu. It was the last aerial combat of World War II. Moore is shown here on his Hellcat after returning to the ship. (MNA)

5

POST VJ-DAY SCENES

Various Japanese Air Force and Navy squadrons engaged the Allies right up to the surrender declaration on 15 August 1945. It had been thought that the assault on Japan by both land and shore-based aviation had seriously depleted enemy air strength. Once ashore, occupying forces discovered that through clever camouflage and dispersal, sometimes five miles from airfields, the Japanese had husbanded a force of some eight thousand aircraft in anticipation of the invasion. The carnage that these units could have caused among the invasion fleet can only be imagined.

Other Japanese aviation units,in Korea, China, Malaya, the Dutch East Indies, as far flung as Rabaul, surrendered an additional 2,000 aircraft. Only in the final months of the war had Japanese aircraft manufacturing been seriously interrupted by bombing. A lack of fuel and skilled aircrews had posed greater problems.

These scenes were recorded immediately after VJ-Day when the guns had gone silent. They give a sense of the finality, the scope of the destruction, and the air forces that were still arrayed had the conflict continued.

A junk yard of aircraft wrecks on Eaton Island, Truk, is seen from a Navy recon aircraft in August 1945. (MNA)

Above: A Japanese Mitsubishi G4M Betty bore the Japanese truce delegation to Ie Shima. The escort, a trio of multi-gun Mitchells from the 345th Bomb Group are seen overhead. Armed guards lined the runway and every American soldier on the island watched the event. (Author's Collection)

Below: The Betty, bearing green crosses rather than the Japanese insignia, taxiied to a hard stand. (Author's Collection)

Above: The truce team of senior officers and diplomats approach a C-54 for the trip to Manila and a meeting with General MacArthur to discuss surrender arrangements. (Author's Collection)

Below: The Betty's crew wait awkwardly under the wing of their aircraft. (Author's Collection)

Above: Photo reconnaissance had pinpointed Allied POW camps in Japan. Here a B-29 buzzes Omori on Tokyo Bay shortly after the surrender. (Hap Halloran)

Below: Supplies were air dropped and the prisoners initiated communications by painting signs on the roof of compound buildings. The one at far right advises: "Pappy Boyington here!," referring to Major Gregory Boyington, the Marine ace who had been listed as missing near Rabaul since January 1944. (Hap Halloran)

Above: Although surrounded and isolated since early 1944, the garrison at Rabaul maintained a handful of aircraft until the August 1945 surrender. Here is one of the Guerrilla Air Force, an A6M, Model 22, surrendered to New Zealand forces. (C. Darby via Jim Lansdale)

Below: A very war weary Mitsubishi Zeke, with center-point ordnance rack, rests on a Japanese airfield after the surrender. (Author's Collection)

Above: A Grumman Avenger from H.M.S. *Indomitable* lands at Kai Tek airfield, Hong Kong after the Japanese surrender and is viewed by friend and foe alike. Note the flat tire. (Jerry Scutts)

Right: Lieutenant Colonel Phil Rasmussen, who had downed a Japanese attacker over Oahu on 7 December 1941, inspects a Mitsubishi J2M Jack at Atsugi Airdrome. He had flown nearly 200 combat missions in the Southwest Pacific and the final Western Pacific campaign. By terms of the surrender agreement propellors were being removed from Japanese aircraft to assure that they were inoperable. (Author's Collection)

Harbors and bays on Japan's Inland Sea were littered with the wrecks of the Imperial fleet, sunk by Allied aerial attacks. Here are just two examples:

Above: Heavy cruiser *Tone* is pictured after the surrender, upright but on the bottom, off Eta Jima Island. She succumbed to six direct hits and 14 near misses, all administered by Task Force 38 attackers on 24 and 28 July 1945. (USN)

Below: The new Japanese aircraft carrier *Amagi* was completed in August 1944 but never sailed into battle due to a shortage of escort vessels, trained carrier pilots, and finally a lack of fuel. She was first hit by carrier based aircraft on 19 March 1945 and then again on 28 July. Numerous near misses caused her to capsize and roll on her side in shallow water near Kurahashi Jima. (USAF via USN)

Atsugi Airdrome, near Yokahama, was soon a graveyard of Japanese warbirds.

Above: A collection of Mitsubishi Zekes with props removed. (Author's Collection)

Below: An AAF pilot inspects a Mitsubishi J2M Raiden (Jack). (Author's Collection)

Above: 1st Lieutenant Jim Weir, a 318th Fighter Group pilot, stands by an Aichi D3A Val at Atsugi. Less than a month earlier he had downed a Val near Kyushu.(Jim Weir)

Below: The Nakajima G5N Shinzan (Liz to the Allies) was Japan's belated effort at producing a long-range strategic bomber. Beset by engine problems, only four were built and none saw action. (Author's Collection)

Japanese fortunes had sunk so low that even ancient biplanes had been used against the Allied fleet near Okinawa. Although their success rate was nil, those that might survive flak and fighters during an invasion of Japan could have caused grave casualties among landing craft.

Above: A fabric-covered Type 93 trainer. (Author's Collection)

Below: A Nakajima Type 95 reconnaissance seaplane found near Yokosuka, minus its entire right wing section. (Author's Collection)

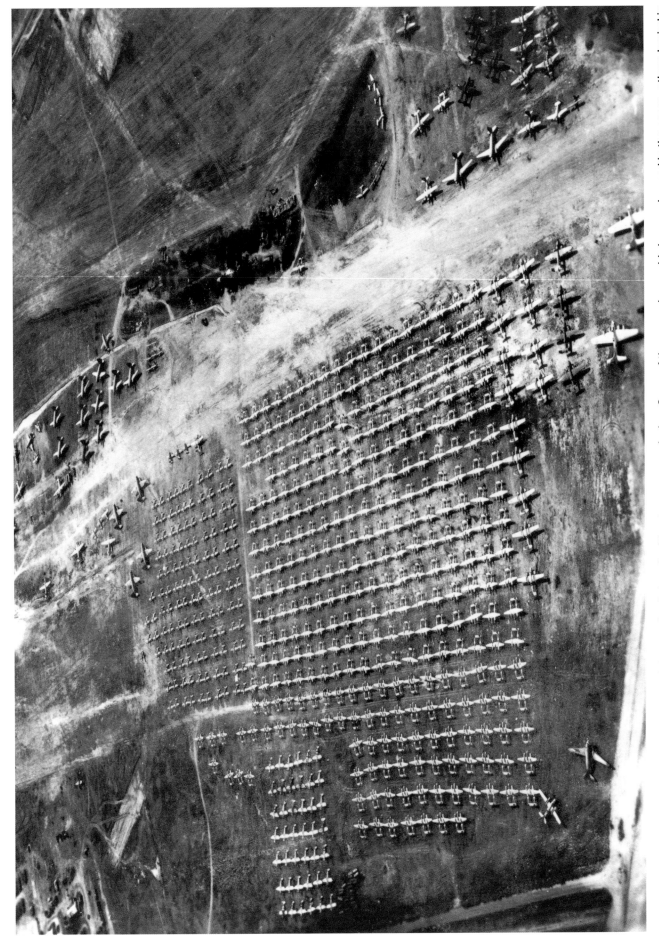

With hostilities ended, the US Army Air Force had thousands of aircraft without crews or a mission. Some of these surplus warbirds were dumped in the ocean, others buried in the soft ash of Iwo Jima. Many, like those above, were flown to Clark Field, Luzon awaiting their fate. B-17s, C-47s, A-20s, B-25s, A-26s, P-47s, P-51s and a forest of P-38s can be seen here. Most were largely abandoned and ultimately reduced to scrap — swords into plowshares as it were. (Bill Webster)

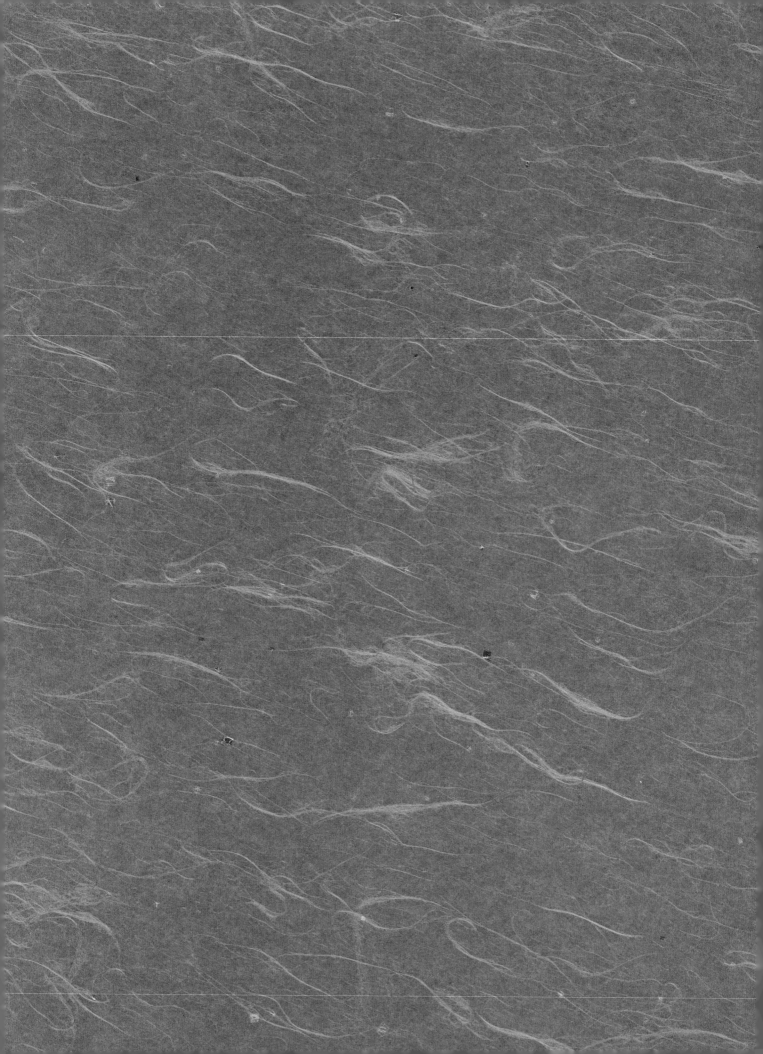